This letters to my Mom in heaven

IS DEDICATED TO:

_____

DEDICATION

This book is dedicated to all the ones who have lost a mom out there.

You are my inspiration in producing books especially when the words will not come.

HOW TO USE THIS LETTERS TO MY MOM IN HEAVEN DIARY:

The purpose of this Letters to My Mom is to keep all your various heart feels and thoughts organized in one easy to find spot.

Here are some simple guidelines to follow so you can make the most of using this book:

1. The first "Dear Mom, I Wanted To Call You Today And Tell You" section is for you to write out what you want to say to your mom, how you felt. So you can go back there to be reminded of your journey...

2. Most ideas are inspired by something we have seen. Use the "This Is What Heaven Will Be Like When We Are Together" section to write down all the things you wish about that day will be like...

3. The "This Is What I Imagine You Doing Up In Heaven Right Now" section is for you to write out all the things you imagine mom doing and recording your journey of loss...

4. And even more pages with the "When We Meet Up in Heaven Again, The First Thing We Will Do Is" section is great for writing out the plans you wish and dream to be doing with mom...

5. The "Today I Am Really Missing" section is for you to keep a visual reminder of each dream you have for things and plans you have when you are reunited in heaven...

6. The "I Am Having A Hard Time With" section is for you to describe your struggles and heart hurts with loss of mom...

7. The "The Hardest Time of Day Is" section is for you to write out the time of day you feel down or depressed about missing mom and, any heart feels especially helpful for remembering later on...

8. The "I Have Been Feeling A Lot Of" section is for you to write out keepsake memories of how you're feeling about missing your mom, your story, your journey so your heart feels listened to...

9. Use this "I Could Use Some More" section as the place to lay out your plan of what you could use more of at this sorrowful time of loss and so your heart will feel understood... And much more!

Whether you've just lost your mom, or it's been years now...you will want to write down all your heart feels in this notebook to look back on and always remember the things you want to say to your Mom in heaven.

LETTERS TO MY *Mom* IN HEAVEN

Dear Mom, I wanted to call you today and tell you...

This is what heaven will be like when we are together...

This is what I imagine you doing up in heaven right now...

When we meet up in heaven again, the first thing we will do is...

Today, I am really missing...

I am having a hard time with...

The hardest time of day is...

I have been feeling a lot of...

LETTERS TO MY *Mom* IN HEAVEN

I could use some more...

I could use a little less...

I am ready to feel...

A simple activity or non-activity I could try today to make things easier is...

If I were to ask for help, who might I ask and what would I ask for specifically?

My support system includes...

I find it helpful when...

And I imagine right now your job in heaven is...

Some lessons I learned from knowing you are...

LETTERS TO MY *Mom* IN HEAVEN

On your birthday I will honor you by...

When I get sad cause I miss you, I do this...

One secret that I never told you is...

I feel most connected to my mom when I....

A comforting memory of my mom is...

My faith has changed in these ways...

I want to share this bible verse with you...

Notes

LETTERS TO MY *Mom* IN HEAVEN

LETTERS TO MY *Mom* IN HEAVEN

Dear Mom, I wanted to call you today and tell you...

This is what heaven will be like when we are together...

This is what I imagine you doing up in heaven right now...

When we meet up in heaven again, the first thing we will do is...

Today, I am really missing...

I am having a hard time with...

The hardest time of day is...

I have been feeling a lot of...

LETTERS TO MY *Mom* IN HEAVEN

I could use some more...

I could use a little less...

I am ready to feel...

A simple activity or non-activity I could try today to make things easier is...

If I were to ask for help, who might I ask and what would I ask for specifically?

My support system includes...

I find it helpful when...

And I imagine right now your job in heaven is...

Some lessons I learned from knowing you are...

LETTERS TO MY *Mom* IN HEAVEN

On your birthday I will honor you by...

When I get sad cause I miss you, I do this...

One secret that I never told you is...

I feel most connected to my mom when I....

A comforting memory of my mom is...

My faith has changed in these ways...

I want to share this bible verse with you...

Notes

LETTERS TO MY *Mom* IN HEAVEN

LETTERS TO MY *Mom* IN HEAVEN

Dear Mom, I wanted to call you today and tell you...

This is what heaven will be like when we are together...

This is what I imagine you doing up in heaven right now...

When we meet up in heaven again, the first thing we will do is...

Today, I am really missing...

I am having a hard time with...

The hardest time of day is...

I have been feeling a lot of...

LETTERS TO MY *Mom* IN HEAVEN

I could use some more...

I could use a little less...

I am ready to feel...

A simple activity or non-activity I could try today to make things easier is...

If I were to ask for help, who might I ask and what would I ask for specifically?

My support system includes...

I find it helpful when...

And I imagine right now your job in heaven is...

Some lessons I learned from knowing you are...

LETTERS TO MY *Mom* IN HEAVEN

On your birthday I will honor you by...

When I get sad cause I miss you, I do this...

One secret that I never told you is...

I feel most connected to my mom when I....

A comforting memory of my mom is...

My faith has changed in these ways...

I want to share this bible verse with you...

Notes

LETTERS TO MY *Mom* IN HEAVEN

LETTERS TO MY *Mom* IN HEAVEN

Dear Mom, I wanted to call you today and tell you...

This is what heaven will be like when we are together...

This is what I imagine you doing up in heaven right now...

When we meet up in heaven again, the first thing we will do is...

Today, I am really missing...

I am having a hard time with...

The hardest time of day is...

I have been feeling a lot of...

LETTERS TO MY *Mom* IN HEAVEN

I could use some more...

I could use a little less...

I am ready to feel...

A simple activity or non-activity I could try today to make things easier is...

If I were to ask for help, who might I ask and what would I ask for specifically?

My support system includes...

I find it helpful when...

And I imagine right now your job in heaven is...

Some lessons I learned from knowing you are...

LETTERS TO MY *Mom* IN HEAVEN

On your birthday I will honor you by...

When I get sad cause I miss you, I do this...

One secret that I never told you is...

I feel most connected to my mom when I....

A comforting memory of my mom is...

My faith has changed in these ways...

I want to share this bible verse with you...

Notes

LETTERS TO MY *Mom* IN HEAVEN

LETTERS TO MY *Mom* IN HEAVEN

Dear Mom, I wanted to call you today and tell you...

This is what heaven will be like when we are together...

This is what I imagine you doing up in heaven right now...

When we meet up in heaven again, the first thing we will do is...

Today, I am really missing...

I am having a hard time with...

The hardest time of day is...

I have been feeling a lot of...

LETTERS TO MY *Mom* IN HEAVEN

I could use some more...

I could use a little less...

I am ready to feel...

A simple activity or non-activity I could try today to make things easier is...

If I were to ask for help, who might I ask and what would I ask for specifically?

My support system includes...

I find it helpful when...

And I imagine right now your job in heaven is...

Some lessons I learned from knowing you are...

LETTERS TO MY Mom IN HEAVEN

On your birthday I will honor you by...

When I get sad cause I miss you, I do this...

One secret that I never told you is...

I feel most connected to my mom when I....

A comforting memory of my mom is...

My faith has changed in these ways...

I want to share this bible verse with you...

Notes

LETTERS TO MY *Mom* IN HEAVEN

LETTERS TO MY *Mom* IN HEAVEN

Dear Mom, I wanted to call you today and tell you...

This is what heaven will be like when we are together...

This is what I imagine you doing up in heaven right now...

When we meet up in heaven again, the first thing we will do is...

Today, I am really missing...

I am having a hard time with...

The hardest time of day is...

I have been feeling a lot of...

LETTERS TO MY *Mom* IN HEAVEN

I could use some more...

I could use a little less...

I am ready to feel...

A simple activity or non-activity I could try today to make things easier is...

If I were to ask for help, who might I ask and what would I ask for specifically?

My support system includes...

I find it helpful when...

And I imagine right now your job in heaven is...

Some lessons I learned from knowing you are...

LETTERS TO MY *Mom* IN HEAVEN

On your birthday I will honor you by...

When I get sad cause I miss you, I do this...

One secret that I never told you is...

I feel most connected to my mom when I....

A comforting memory of my mom is...

My faith has changed in these ways...

I want to share this bible verse with you...

Notes

LETTERS TO MY *Mom* IN HEAVEN

LETTERS TO MY *Mom* IN HEAVEN

Dear Mom, I wanted to call you today and tell you...

This is what heaven will be like when we are together...

This is what I imagine you doing up in heaven right now...

When we meet up in heaven again, the first thing we will do is...

Today, I am really missing...

I am having a hard time with...

The hardest time of day is...

I have been feeling a lot of...

LETTERS TO MY Mom IN HEAVEN

I could use some more...

I could use a little less...

I am ready to feel...

A simple activity or non-activity I could try today to make things easier is...

If I were to ask for help, who might I ask and what would I ask for specifically?

My support system includes...

I find it helpful when...

And I imagine right now your job in heaven is...

Some lessons I learned from knowing you are...

LETTERS TO MY *Mom* IN HEAVEN

On your birthday I will honor you by...

When I get sad cause I miss you, I do this...

One secret that I never told you is...

I feel most connected to my mom when I....

A comforting memory of my mom is...

My faith has changed in these ways...

I want to share this bible verse with you...

Notes

LETTERS TO MY *Mom* IN HEAVEN

# LETTERS TO MY *Mom* IN HEAVEN

Dear Mom, I wanted to call you today and tell you...

This is what heaven will be like when we are together...

This is what I imagine you doing up in heaven right now...

When we meet up in heaven again, the first thing we will do is...

Today, I am really missing...

I am having a hard time with...

The hardest time of day is...

I have been feeling a lot of...

LETTERS TO MY *Mom* IN HEAVEN

I could use some more...

I could use a little less...

I am ready to feel...

A simple activity or non-activity I could try today to make things easier is...

If I were to ask for help, who might I ask and what would I ask for specifically?

My support system includes...

I find it helpful when...

And I imagine right now your job in heaven is...

Some lessons I learned from knowing you are...

LETTERS TO MY *Mom* IN HEAVEN

On your birthday I will honor you by...

When I get sad cause I miss you, I do this...

One secret that I never told you is...

I feel most connected to my mom when I....

A comforting memory of my mom is...

My faith has changed in these ways...

I want to share this bible verse with you...

Notes

LETTERS TO MY *Mom* IN HEAVEN

LETTERS TO MY *Mom* IN HEAVEN

Dear Mom, I wanted to call you today and tell you...

This is what heaven will be like when we are together...

This is what I imagine you doing up in heaven right now...

When we meet up in heaven again, the first thing we will do is...

Today, I am really missing...

I am having a hard time with...

The hardest time of day is...

I have been feeling a lot of...

LETTERS TO MY *Mom* IN HEAVEN

I could use some more...

I could use a little less...

I am ready to feel...

A simple activity or non-activity I could try today to make things easier is...

If I were to ask for help, who might I ask and what would I ask for specifically?

My support system includes...

I find it helpful when...

And I imagine right now your job in heaven is...

Some lessons I learned from knowing you are...

LETTERS TO MY *Mom* IN HEAVEN

On your birthday I will honor you by...

When I get sad cause I miss you, I do this...

One secret that I never told you is...

I feel most connected to my mom when I....

A comforting memory of my mom is...

My faith has changed in these ways...

I want to share this bible verse with you...

Notes

LETTERS TO MY *Mom* IN HEAVEN

LETTERS TO MY *Mom* IN HEAVEN

Dear Mom, I wanted to call you today and tell you...

This is what heaven will be like when we are together...

This is what I imagine you doing up in heaven right now...

When we meet up in heaven again, the first thing we will do is...

Today, I am really missing...

I am having a hard time with...

The hardest time of day is...

I have been feeling a lot of...

LETTERS TO MY *Mom* IN HEAVEN

I could use some more...

I could use a little less...

I am ready to feel...

A simple activity or non-activity I could try today to make things easier is...

If I were to ask for help, who might I ask and what would I ask for specifically?

My support system includes...

I find it helpful when...

And I imagine right now your job in heaven is...

Some lessons I learned from knowing you are...

LETTERS TO MY *Mom* IN HEAVEN

On your birthday I will honor you by...

When I get sad cause I miss you, I do this...

One secret that I never told you is...

I feel most connected to my mom when I....

A comforting memory of my mom is...

My faith has changed in these ways...

I want to share this bible verse with you...

Notes

LETTERS TO MY *Mom* IN HEAVEN

LETTERS TO MY *Mom* IN HEAVEN

Dear Mom, I wanted to call you today and tell you...

This is what heaven will be like when we are together...

This is what I imagine you doing up in heaven right now...

When we meet up in heaven again, the first thing we will do is...

Today, I am really missing...

I am having a hard time with...

The hardest time of day is...

I have been feeling a lot of...

LETTERS TO MY *Mom* IN HEAVEN

I could use some more...

I could use a little less...

I am ready to feel...

A simple activity or non-activity I could try today to make things easier is...

If I were to ask for help, who might I ask and what would I ask for specifically?

My support system includes...

I find it helpful when...

And I imagine right now your job in heaven is...

Some lessons I learned from knowing you are...

LETTERS TO MY *Mom* IN HEAVEN

On your birthday I will honor you by...

When I get sad cause I miss you, I do this...

One secret that I never told you is...

I feel most connected to my mom when I....

A comforting memory of my mom is...

My faith has changed in these ways...

I want to share this bible verse with you...

Notes

LETTERS TO MY *Mom* IN HEAVEN

LETTERS TO MY *Mom* IN HEAVEN

Dear Mom, I wanted to call you today and tell you...

This is what heaven will be like when we are together...

This is what I imagine you doing up in heaven right now...

When we meet up in heaven again, the first thing we will do is...

Today, I am really missing...

I am having a hard time with...

The hardest time of day is...

I have been feeling a lot of...

LETTERS TO MY *Mom* IN HEAVEN

I could use some more...

I could use a little less...

I am ready to feel...

A simple activity or non-activity I could try today to make things easier is...

If I were to ask for help, who might I ask and what would I ask for specifically?

My support system includes...

I find it helpful when...

And I imagine right now your job in heaven is...

Some lessons I learned from knowing you are...

LETTERS TO MY *Mom* IN HEAVEN

On your birthday I will honor you by...

When I get sad cause I miss you, I do this...

One secret that I never told you is...

I feel most connected to my mom when I....

A comforting memory of my mom is...

My faith has changed in these ways...

I want to share this bible verse with you...

Notes

LETTERS TO MY *Mom* IN HEAVEN

LETTERS TO MY *Mom* IN HEAVEN

Dear Mom, I wanted to call you today and tell you...

This is what heaven will be like when we are together...

This is what I imagine you doing up in heaven right now...

When we meet up in heaven again, the first thing we will do is...

Today, I am really missing...

I am having a hard time with...

The hardest time of day is...

I have been feeling a lot of...

LETTERS TO MY *Mom* IN HEAVEN

I could use some more...

I could use a little less...

I am ready to feel...

A simple activity or non-activity I could try today to make things easier is...

If I were to ask for help, who might I ask and what would I ask for specifically?

My support system includes...

I find it helpful when...

And I imagine right now your job in heaven is...

Some lessons I learned from knowing you are...

LETTERS TO MY *Mom* IN HEAVEN

On your birthday I will honor you by...

When I get sad cause I miss you, I do this...

One secret that I never told you is...

I feel most connected to my mom when I....

A comforting memory of my mom is...

My faith has changed in these ways...

I want to share this bible verse with you...

Notes

LETTERS TO MY *Mom* IN HEAVEN

LETTERS TO MY *Mom* IN HEAVEN

Dear Mom, I wanted to call you today and tell you...

This is what heaven will be like when we are together...

This is what I imagine you doing up in heaven right now...

When we meet up in heaven again, the first thing we will do is...

Today, I am really missing...

I am having a hard time with...

The hardest time of day is...

I have been feeling a lot of...

LETTERS TO MY *Mom* IN HEAVEN

I could use some more...

I could use a little less...

I am ready to feel...

A simple activity or non-activity I could try today to make things easier is...

If I were to ask for help, who might I ask and what would I ask for specifically?

My support system includes...

I find it helpful when...

And I imagine right now your job in heaven is...

Some lessons I learned from knowing you are...

LETTERS TO MY *Mom* IN HEAVEN

On your birthday I will honor you by...

When I get sad cause I miss you, I do this...

One secret that I never told you is...

I feel most connected to my mom when I....

A comforting memory of my mom is...

My faith has changed in these ways...

I want to share this bible verse with you...

Notes

LETTERS TO MY *Mom* IN HEAVEN

LETTERS TO MY *Mom* IN HEAVEN

Dear Mom, I wanted to call you today and tell you...

This is what heaven will be like when we are together...

This is what I imagine you doing up in heaven right now...

When we meet up in heaven again, the first thing we will do is...

Today, I am really missing...

I am having a hard time with...

The hardest time of day is...

I have been feeling a lot of...

LETTERS TO MY *Mom* IN HEAVEN

I could use some more...

I could use a little less...

I am ready to feel...

A simple activity or non-activity I could try today to make things easier is...

If I were to ask for help, who might I ask and what would I ask for specifically?

My support system includes...

I find it helpful when...

And I imagine right now your job in heaven is...

Some lessons I learned from knowing you are...

LETTERS TO MY *Mom* IN HEAVEN

On your birthday I will honor you by...

When I get sad cause I miss you, I do this...

One secret that I never told you is...

I feel most connected to my mom when I....

A comforting memory of my mom is...

My faith has changed in these ways...

I want to share this bible verse with you...

Notes

LETTERS TO MY *Mom* IN HEAVEN

LETTERS TO MY *Mom* IN HEAVEN

Dear Mom, I wanted to call you today and tell you...

This is what heaven will be like when we are together...

This is what I imagine you doing up in heaven right now...

When we meet up in heaven again, the first thing we will do is...

Today, I am really missing...

I am having a hard time with...

The hardest time of day is...

I have been feeling a lot of...

LETTERS TO MY *Mom* IN HEAVEN

I could use some more...

_____

I could use a little less...

_____

I am ready to feel...

_____

A simple activity or non-activity I could try today to make things easier is...

_____

If I were to ask for help, who might I ask and what would I ask for specifically?

_____

My support system includes...

_____

I find it helpful when...

_____

And I imagine right now your job in heaven is...

_____

Some lessons I learned from knowing you are...

_____

LETTERS TO MY *Mom* IN HEAVEN

On your birthday I will honor you by...

When I get sad cause I miss you, I do this...

One secret that I never told you is...

I feel most connected to my mom when I....

A comforting memory of my mom is...

My faith has changed in these ways...

I want to share this bible verse with you...

Notes

LETTERS TO MY *Mom* IN HEAVEN

LETTERS TO MY *Mom* IN HEAVEN

Dear Mom, I wanted to call you today and tell you...

This is what heaven will be like when we are together...

This is what I imagine you doing up in heaven right now...

When we meet up in heaven again, the first thing we will do is...

Today, I am really missing...

I am having a hard time with...

The hardest time of day is...

I have been feeling a lot of...

LETTERS TO MY *Mom* IN HEAVEN

I could use some more...

I could use a little less...

I am ready to feel...

A simple activity or non-activity I could try today to make things easier is...

If I were to ask for help, who might I ask and what would I ask for specifically?

My support system includes...

I find it helpful when...

And I imagine right now your job in heaven is...

Some lessons I learned from knowing you are...

LETTERS TO MY *Mom* IN HEAVEN

On your birthday I will honor you by...

When I get sad cause I miss you, I do this...

One secret that I never told you is...

I feel most connected to my mom when I....

A comforting memory of my mom is...

My faith has changed in these ways...

I want to share this bible verse with you...

Notes

LETTERS TO MY *Mom* IN HEAVEN

LETTERS TO MY *Mom* IN HEAVEN

Dear Mom, I wanted to call you today and tell you...

This is what heaven will be like when we are together...

This is what I imagine you doing up in heaven right now...

When we meet up in heaven again, the first thing we will do is...

Today, I am really missing...

I am having a hard time with...

The hardest time of day is...

I have been feeling a lot of...

LETTERS TO MY *Mom* IN HEAVEN

I could use some more...

I could use a little less...

I am ready to feel...

A simple activity or non-activity I could try today to make things easier is...

If I were to ask for help, who might I ask and what would I ask for specifically?

My support system includes...

I find it helpful when...

And I imagine right now your job in heaven is...

Some lessons I learned from knowing you are...

LETTERS TO MY *Mom* IN HEAVEN

On your birthday I will honor you by...

When I get sad cause I miss you, I do this...

One secret that I never told you is...

I feel most connected to my mom when I....

A comforting memory of my mom is...

My faith has changed in these ways...

I want to share this bible verse with you...

Notes

LETTERS TO MY *Mom* IN HEAVEN

LETTERS TO MY *Mom* IN HEAVEN

Dear Mom, I wanted to call you today and tell you...

This is what heaven will be like when we are together...

This is what I imagine you doing up in heaven right now...

When we meet up in heaven again, the first thing we will do is...

Today, I am really missing...

I am having a hard time with...

The hardest time of day is...

I have been feeling a lot of...

LETTERS TO MY *Mom* IN HEAVEN

I could use some more...

I could use a little less...

I am ready to feel...

A simple activity or non-activity I could try today to make things easier is...

If I were to ask for help, who might I ask and what would I ask for specifically?

My support system includes...

I find it helpful when...

And I imagine right now your job in heaven is...

Some lessons I learned from knowing you are...

LETTERS TO MY *Mom* IN HEAVEN

On your birthday I will honor you by...

When I get sad cause I miss you, I do this...

One secret that I never told you is...

I feel most connected to my mom when I....

A comforting memory of my mom is...

My faith has changed in these ways...

I want to share this bible verse with you...

Notes

LETTERS TO MY *Mom* IN HEAVEN

LETTERS TO MY *Mom* IN HEAVEN

Dear Mom, I wanted to call you today and tell you...

This is what heaven will be like when we are together...

This is what I imagine you doing up in heaven right now...

When we meet up in heaven again, the first thing we will do is...

Today, I am really missing...

I am having a hard time with...

The hardest time of day is...

I have been feeling a lot of...

LETTERS TO MY *Mom* IN HEAVEN

I could use some more...

I could use a little less...

I am ready to feel...

A simple activity or non-activity I could try today to make things easier is...

If I were to ask for help, who might I ask and what would I ask for specifically?

My support system includes...

I find it helpful when...

And I imagine right now your job in heaven is...

Some lessons I learned from knowing you are...

LETTERS TO MY *Mom* IN HEAVEN

On your birthday I will honor you by...

When I get sad cause I miss you, I do this...

One secret that I never told you is...

I feel most connected to my mom when I....

A comforting memory of my mom is...

My faith has changed in these ways...

I want to share this bible verse with you...

Notes

LETTERS TO MY *Mom* IN HEAVEN

LETTERS TO MY *Mom* IN HEAVEN

Dear Mom, I wanted to call you today and tell you...

This is what heaven will be like when we are together...

This is what I imagine you doing up in heaven right now...

When we meet up in heaven again, the first thing we will do is...

Today, I am really missing...

I am having a hard time with...

The hardest time of day is...

I have been feeling a lot of...

LETTERS TO MY *Mom* IN HEAVEN

I could use some more...

I could use a little less...

I am ready to feel...

A simple activity or non-activity I could try today to make things easier is...

If I were to ask for help, who might I ask and what would I ask for specifically?

My support system includes...

I find it helpful when...

And I imagine right now your job in heaven is...

Some lessons I learned from knowing you are...

LETTERS TO MY *Mom* IN HEAVEN

On your birthday I will honor you by...

When I get sad cause I miss you, I do this...

One secret that I never told you is...

I feel most connected to my mom when I....

A comforting memory of my mom is...

My faith has changed in these ways...

I want to share this bible verse with you...

Notes

LETTERS TO MY *Mom* IN HEAVEN

LETTERS TO MY *Mom* IN HEAVEN

Dear Mom, I wanted to call you today and tell you...

This is what heaven will be like when we are together...

This is what I imagine you doing up in heaven right now...

When we meet up in heaven again, the first thing we will do is...

Today, I am really missing...

I am having a hard time with...

The hardest time of day is...

I have been feeling a lot of...

LETTERS TO MY *Mom* IN HEAVEN

I could use some more...

I could use a little less...

I am ready to feel...

A simple activity or non-activity I could try today to make things easier is...

If I were to ask for help, who might I ask and what would I ask for specifically?

My support system includes...

I find it helpful when...

And I imagine right now your job in heaven is...

Some lessons I learned from knowing you are...

LETTERS TO MY *Mom* IN HEAVEN

On your birthday I will honor you by...

When I get sad cause I miss you, I do this...

One secret that I never told you is...

I feel most connected to my mom when I....

A comforting memory of my mom is...

My faith has changed in these ways...

I want to share this bible verse with you...

Notes

LETTERS TO MY *Mom* IN HEAVEN

LETTERS TO MY *Mom* IN HEAVEN

Dear Mom, I wanted to call you today and tell you...

This is what heaven will be like when we are together...

This is what I imagine you doing up in heaven right now...

When we meet up in heaven again, the first thing we will do is...

Today, I am really missing...

I am having a hard time with...

The hardest time of day is...

I have been feeling a lot of...

# LETTERS TO MY *Mom* IN HEAVEN

I could use some more...

I could use a little less...

I am ready to feel...

A simple activity or non-activity I could try today to make things easier is...

If I were to ask for help, who might I ask and what would I ask for specifically?

My support system includes...

I find it helpful when...

And I imagine right now your job in heaven is...

Some lessons I learned from knowing you are...

LETTERS TO MY *Mom* IN HEAVEN

On your birthday I will honor you by...

When I get sad cause I miss you, I do this...

One secret that I never told you is...

I feel most connected to my mom when I....

A comforting memory of my mom is...

My faith has changed in these ways...

I want to share this bible verse with you...

Notes

LETTERS TO MY *Mom* IN HEAVEN

LETTERS TO MY *Mom* IN HEAVEN

Dear Mom, I wanted to call you today and tell you...

This is what heaven will be like when we are together...

This is what I imagine you doing up in heaven right now...

When we meet up in heaven again, the first thing we will do is...

Today, I am really missing...

I am having a hard time with...

The hardest time of day is...

I have been feeling a lot of...

LETTERS TO MY *Mom* IN HEAVEN

I could use some more...

I could use a little less...

I am ready to feel...

A simple activity or non-activity I could try today to make things easier is...

If I were to ask for help, who might I ask and what would I ask for specifically?

My support system includes...

I find it helpful when...

And I imagine right now your job in heaven is...

Some lessons I learned from knowing you are...

LETTERS TO MY *Mom* IN HEAVEN

On your birthday I will honor you by...

When I get sad cause I miss you, I do this...

One secret that I never told you is...

I feel most connected to my mom when I....

A comforting memory of my mom is...

My faith has changed in these ways...

I want to share this bible verse with you...

Notes

LETTERS TO MY *Mom* IN HEAVEN

LETTERS TO MY *Mom* IN HEAVEN

Dear Mom, I wanted to call you today and tell you...

This is what heaven will be like when we are together...

This is what I imagine you doing up in heaven right now...

When we meet up in heaven again, the first thing we will do is...

Today, I am really missing...

I am having a hard time with...

The hardest time of day is...

I have been feeling a lot of...

LETTERS TO MY *Mom* IN HEAVEN

I could use some more...

I could use a little less...

I am ready to feel...

A simple activity or non-activity I could try today to make things easier is...

If I were to ask for help, who might I ask and what would I ask for specifically?

My support system includes...

I find it helpful when...

And I imagine right now your job in heaven is...

Some lessons I learned from knowing you are...

LETTERS TO MY *Mom* IN HEAVEN

On your birthday I will honor you by...

When I get sad cause I miss you, I do this...

One secret that I never told you is...

I feel most connected to my mom when I....

A comforting memory of my mom is...

My faith has changed in these ways...

I want to share this bible verse with you...

Notes

LETTERS TO MY *Mom* IN HEAVEN

LETTERS TO MY *Mom* IN HEAVEN

Dear Mom, I wanted to call you today and tell you...

This is what heaven will be like when we are together...

This is what I imagine you doing up in heaven right now...

When we meet up in heaven again, the first thing we will do is...

Today, I am really missing...

I am having a hard time with...

The hardest time of day is...

I have been feeling a lot of...

LETTERS TO MY *Mom* IN HEAVEN

I could use some more...

I could use a little less...

I am ready to feel...

A simple activity or non-activity I could try today to make things easier is...

If I were to ask for help, who might I ask and what would I ask for specifically?

My support system includes...

I find it helpful when...

And I imagine right now your job in heaven is...

Some lessons I learned from knowing you are...

LETTERS TO MY *Mom* IN HEAVEN

On your birthday I will honor you by...

When I get sad cause I miss you, I do this...

One secret that I never told you is...

I feel most connected to my mom when I....

A comforting memory of my mom is...

My faith has changed in these ways...

I want to share this bible verse with you...

Notes

LETTERS TO MY *Mom* IN HEAVEN

LETTERS TO MY *Mom* IN HEAVEN

Dear Mom, I wanted to call you today and tell you...

This is what heaven will be like when we are together...

This is what I imagine you doing up in heaven right now...

When we meet up in heaven again, the first thing we will do is...

Today, I am really missing...

I am having a hard time with...

The hardest time of day is...

I have been feeling a lot of...

LETTERS TO MY *Mom* IN HEAVEN

I could use some more...

I could use a little less...

I am ready to feel...

A simple activity or non-activity I could try today to make things easier is...

If I were to ask for help, who might I ask and what would I ask for specifically?

My support system includes...

I find it helpful when...

And I imagine right now your job in heaven is...

Some lessons I learned from knowing you are...

LETTERS TO MY *Mom* IN HEAVEN

On your birthday I will honor you by...

When I get sad cause I miss you, I do this...

One secret that I never told you is...

I feel most connected to my mom when I....

A comforting memory of my mom is...

My faith has changed in these ways...

I want to share this bible verse with you...

Notes

LETTERS TO MY *Mom* IN HEAVEN

LETTERS TO MY *Mom* IN HEAVEN

Dear Mom, I wanted to call you today and tell you...

This is what heaven will be like when we are together...

This is what I imagine you doing up in heaven right now...

When we meet up in heaven again, the first thing we will do is...

Today, I am really missing...

I am having a hard time with...

The hardest time of day is...

I have been feeling a lot of...

LETTERS TO MY *Mom* IN HEAVEN

I could use some more...

I could use a little less...

I am ready to feel...

A simple activity or non-activity I could try today to make things easier is...

If I were to ask for help, who might I ask and what would I ask for specifically?

My support system includes...

I find it helpful when...

And I imagine right now your job in heaven is...

Some lessons I learned from knowing you are...

LETTERS TO MY *Mom* IN HEAVEN

On your birthday I will honor you by...

When I get sad cause I miss you, I do this...

One secret that I never told you is...

I feel most connected to my mom when I....

A comforting memory of my mom is...

My faith has changed in these ways...

I want to share this bible verse with you...

Notes

LETTERS TO MY *Mom* IN HEAVEN

LETTERS TO MY *Mom* IN HEAVEN

Dear Mom, I wanted to call you today and tell you...

This is what heaven will be like when we are together...

This is what I imagine you doing up in heaven right now...

When we meet up in heaven again, the first thing we will do is...

Today, I am really missing...

I am having a hard time with...

The hardest time of day is...

I have been feeling a lot of...

LETTERS TO MY *Mom* IN HEAVEN

I could use some more...

I could use a little less...

I am ready to feel...

A simple activity or non-activity I could try today to make things easier is...

If I were to ask for help, who might I ask and what would I ask for specifically?

My support system includes...

I find it helpful when...

And I imagine right now your job in heaven is...

Some lessons I learned from knowing you are...

LETTERS TO MY *Mom* IN HEAVEN

On your birthday I will honor you by...

When I get sad cause I miss you, I do this...

One secret that I never told you is...

I feel most connected to my mom when I....

A comforting memory of my mom is...

My faith has changed in these ways...

I want to share this bible verse with you...

Notes

LETTERS TO MY *Mom* IN HEAVEN

LETTERS TO MY *Mom* IN HEAVEN

CPSIA information can be obtained
at www.ICGtesting.com
Printed in the USA
LVHW020346100221
678887LV00014B/871